S0-ADX-742

To:

From:

For My Friend

Compiled by
Nick Beilenson

PETER PAUPER PRESS, INC.
WHITE PLAINS, NEW YORK

Text border by
Charles Waller

For Kent, Tom, Fred,
and Lynton

Copyright © 1991, 1995
Peter Pauper Press, Inc.
202 Mamaroneck Avenue
White Plains, NY 10601
All rights reserved
ISBN 0-88088-730-3
Printed in China
30 29 28 27 26 25 24

FOR MY FRIEND

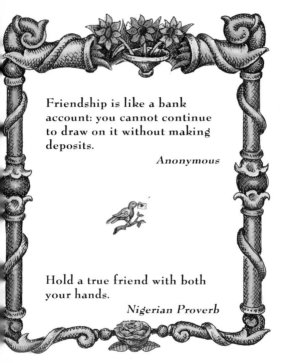

Friendship is like a bank
account: you cannot continue
to draw on it without making
deposits.

Anonymous

Hold a true friend with both
your hands.

Nigerian Proverb

A friend you have to buy won't
be worth what you pay for
him.

George D. Prentice

The surest way to lose a friend
is to tell him something for his
own good.

Sid Ascher

A book is a friend; a good book is a good friend. It will talk to you when you want it to talk, and it will keep still when you want it to keep still—and there are not many friends who know enough to do that. A library is a collection of friends.

Lyman Abbott

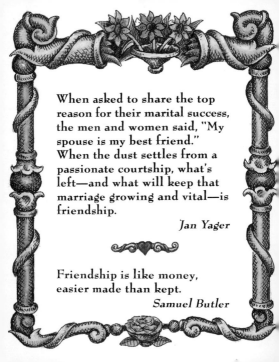

When asked to share the top reason for their marital success, the men and women said, "My spouse is my best friend." When the dust settles from a passionate courtship, what's left—and what will keep that marriage growing and vital—is friendship.

Jan Yager

Friendship is like money, easier made than kept.

Samuel Butler

"Stay" is a charming word in a friend's vocabulary.

Amos Bronson Alcott

Friendship is the hardest thing in the world to explain. It's not something you learn in school. But if you haven't learned the meaning of friendship, you really haven't learned anything.

Muhammad Ali

A doubtful friend is worse than a certain enemy. Let a man be one thing or the other, and we then know how to meet him.

Aesop

Never explain—your friends do not need it, and your enemies will not believe it anyway.

Anonymous

Business, you know, may bring money, but friendship hardly ever does.

Jane Austen

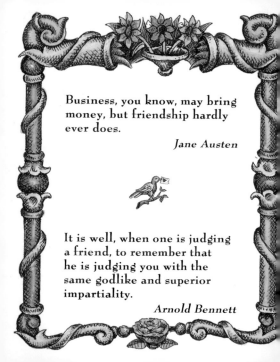

It is well, when one is judging a friend, to remember that he is judging you with the same godlike and superior impartiality.

Arnold Bennett

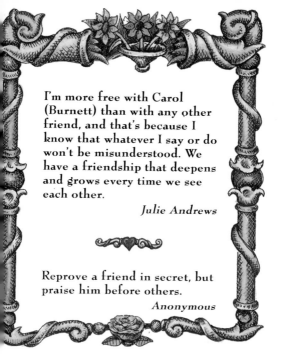

I'm more free with Carol (Burnett) than with any other friend, and that's because I know that whatever I say or do won't be misunderstood. We have a friendship that deepens and grows every time we see each other.

Julie Andrews

Reprove a friend in secret, but praise him before others.

Anonymous

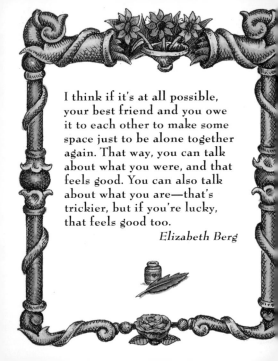

I think if it's at all possible, your best friend and you owe it to each other to make some space just to be alone together again. That way, you can talk about what you were, and that feels good. You can also talk about what you are—that's trickier, but if you're lucky, that feels good too.

Elizabeth Berg

Being a good friend, and having a good friend, can enrich your days and bring you lifelong satisfaction. But friendships don't just happen. They have to be created and nurtured. Like any other skill, building friendship has to be practiced.

Sue Browder

When friends meet, hearts warm.

Proverb

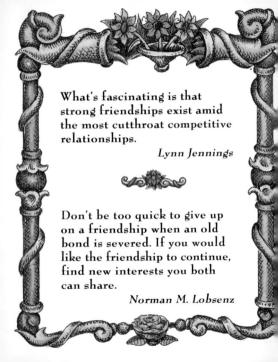

What's fascinating is that strong friendships exist amid the most cutthroat competitive relationships.

Lynn Jennings

Don't be too quick to give up on a friendship when an old bond is severed. If you would like the friendship to continue, find new interests you both can share.

Norman M. Lobsenz

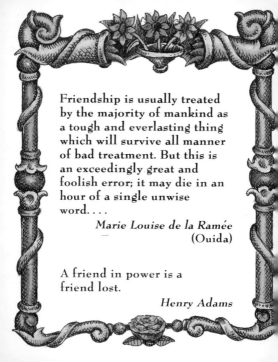

Friendship is usually treated
by the majority of mankind as
a tough and everlasting thing
which will survive all manner
of bad treatment. But this is
an exceedingly great and
foolish error; it may die in an
hour of a single unwise
word. . . .

Marie Louise de la Ramée
(Ouida)

A friend in power is a
friend lost.

Henry Adams

It is better, given the choice,
to have friends.

> *Elizabeth Bishop*,
> explaining why she
> didn't write criticism

If two people do not exist as
separate individuals, then
their friendship is an illusion.

> *Joel Block*

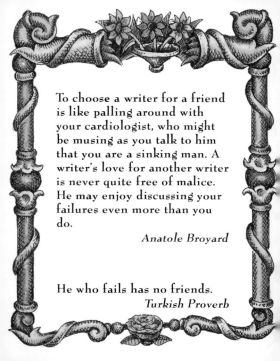

To choose a writer for a friend
is like palling around with
your cardiologist, who might
be musing as you talk to him
that you are a sinking man. A
writer's love for another writer
is never quite free of malice.
He may enjoy discussing your
failures even more than you
do.

Anatole Broyard

He who fails has no friends.

Turkish Proverb

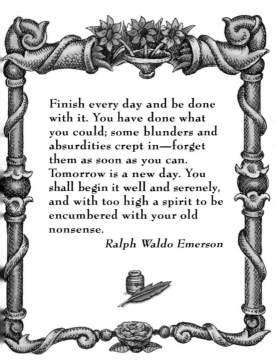

Finish every day and be done with it. You have done what you could; some blunders and absurdities crept in—forget them as soon as you can. Tomorrow is a new day. You shall begin it well and serenely, and with too high a spirit to be encumbered with your old nonsense.

Ralph Waldo Emerson

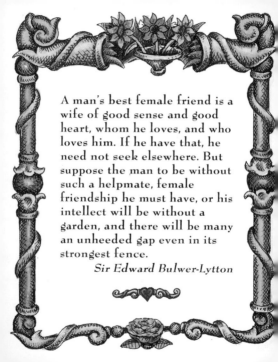

A man's best female friend is a wife of good sense and good heart, whom he loves, and who loves him. If he have that, he need not seek elsewhere. But suppose the man to be without such a helpmate, female friendship he must have, or his intellect will be without a garden, and there will be many an unheeded gap even in its strongest fence.

Sir Edward Bulwer-Lytton

Don't believe your friends when they ask you to be honest with them. All they really want is to be maintained in the good opinion they have of themselves.

Albert Camus

My friend is one whom I can associate with my choicest thoughts.

Henry David Thoreau

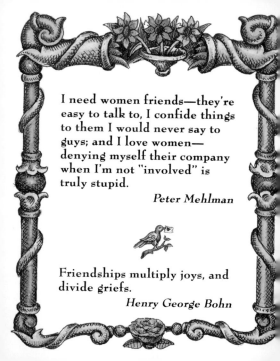

I need women friends—they're easy to talk to, I confide things to them I would never say to guys; and I love women—denying myself their company when I'm not "involved" is truly stupid.

Peter Mehlman

Friendships multiply joys, and divide griefs.

Henry George Bohn

When people realize they can have good close nonsexual relationships with the opposite sex, they may get away from this notion that any adult relationship between the sexes has to end in bed. That's only true in soap operas.

Peter Sheras

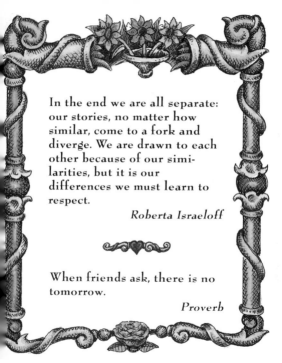

In the end we are all separate:
our stories, no matter how
similar, come to a fork and
diverge. We are drawn to each
other because of our simi-
larities, but it is our
differences we must learn to
respect.

Roberta Israeloff

When friends ask, there is no
tomorrow.

Proverb

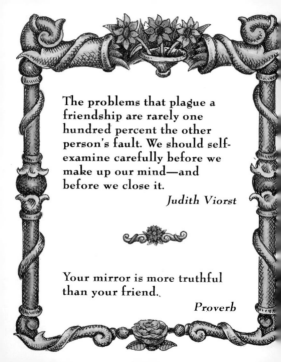

The problems that plague a friendship are rarely one hundred percent the other person's fault. We should self-examine carefully before we make up our mind—and before we close it.

Judith Viorst

Your mirror is more truthful than your friend.

Proverb

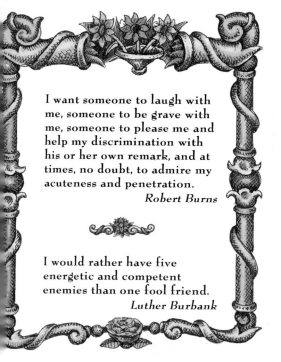

I want someone to laugh with
me, someone to be grave with
me, someone to please me and
help my discrimination with
his or her own remark, and at
times, no doubt, to admire my
acuteness and penetration.

Robert Burns

I would rather have five
energetic and competent
enemies than one fool friend.

Luther Burbank

Friendship is possible only because people do not say to your face the things they say behind your back.

Anonymous

When two friends part they should lock up each other's secrets and exchange keys. The truly noble mind has no resentments.

Diogenes

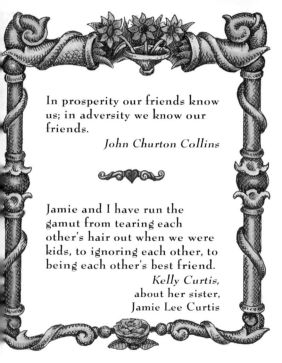

In prosperity our friends know us; in adversity we know our friends.

John Churton Collins

Jamie and I have run the gamut from tearing each other's hair out when we were kids, to ignoring each other, to being each other's best friend.

Kelly Curtis, about her sister, Jamie Lee Curtis

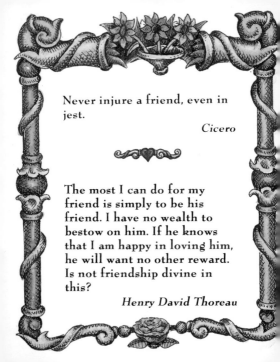

Never injure a friend, even in jest.

Cicero

The most I can do for my friend is simply to be his friend. I have no wealth to bestow on him. If he knows that I am happy in loving him, he will want no other reward. Is not friendship divine in this?

Henry David Thoreau

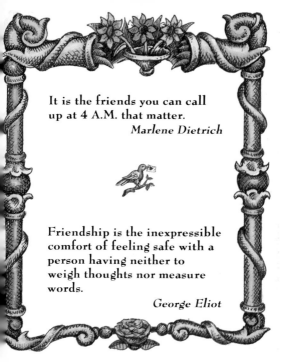

It is the friends you can call
up at 4 A.M. that matter.
Marlene Dietrich

Friendship is the inexpressible
comfort of feeling safe with a
person having neither to
weigh thoughts nor measure
words.

George Eliot

Animals are such agreeable
friends—they ask no questions,
they pass no criticisms.

George Eliot

Friendships begin with liking
or gratitude—roots that can be
pulled up.

George Eliot

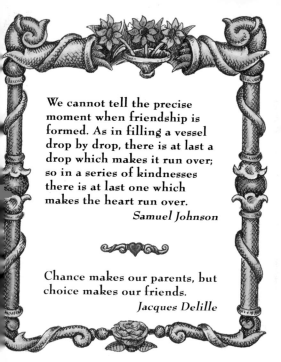

We cannot tell the precise moment when friendship is formed. As in filling a vessel drop by drop, there is at last a drop which makes it run over; so in a series of kindnesses there is at last one which makes the heart run over.

Samuel Johnson

Chance makes our parents, but choice makes our friends.

Jacques Delille

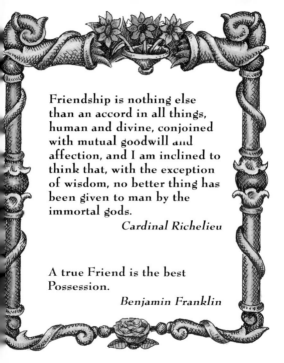

Friendship is nothing else
than an accord in all things,
human and divine, conjoined
with mutual goodwill and
affection, and I am inclined to
think that, with the exception
of wisdom, no better thing has
been given to man by the
immortal gods.

Cardinal Richelieu

A true Friend is the best
Possession.

Benjamin Franklin

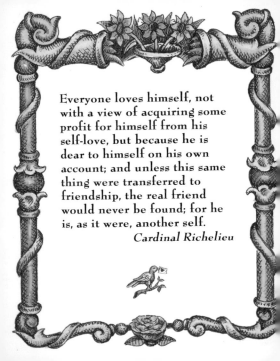

Everyone loves himself, not with a view of acquiring some profit for himself from his self-love, but because he is dear to himself on his own account; and unless this same thing were transferred to friendship, the real friend would never be found; for he is, as it were, another self.

Cardinal Richelieu

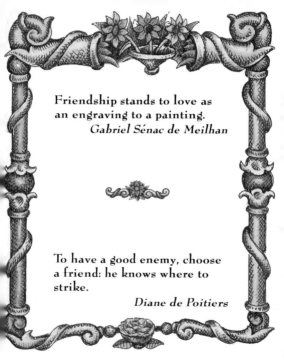

Friendship stands to love as
an engraving to a painting.
Gabriel Sénac de Meilhan

To have a good enemy, choose
a friend: he knows where to
strike.

Diane de Poitiers

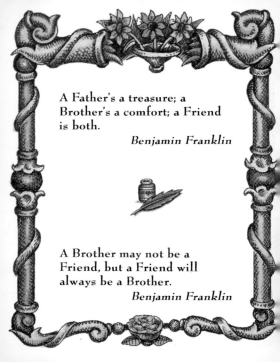

A Father's a treasure; a
Brother's a comfort; a Friend
is both.

Benjamin Franklin

A Brother may not be a
Friend, but a Friend will
always be a Brother.

Benjamin Franklin

Friend who suffereth alone
doth his friend offend.
Jean de Rotrou

It is one of the beautiful
compensations of this life that
no one can sincerely try to
help another without helping
himself.
Charles Dudley Warner

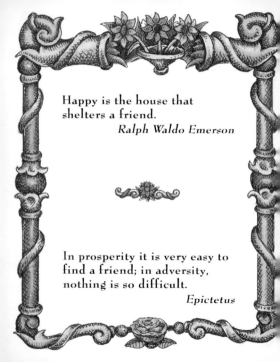

Happy is the house that
shelters a friend.
Ralph Waldo Emerson

In prosperity it is very easy to
find a friend; in adversity,
nothing is so difficult.
Epictetus

No man can be happy without
a friend, nor be sure of his
friend till he is unhappy.
Thomas Fuller

True friendship comes when
silence between two people is
comfortable.
Dave Tyson Gentry

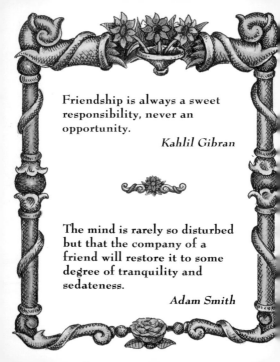

Friendship is always a sweet responsibility, never an opportunity.

Kahlil Gibran

The mind is rarely so disturbed but that the company of a friend will restore it to some degree of tranquility and sedateness.

Adam Smith

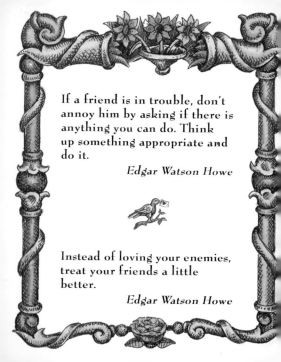

If a friend is in trouble, don't annoy him by asking if there is anything you can do. Think up something appropriate and do it.

Edgar Watson Howe

Instead of loving your enemies, treat your friends a little better.

Edgar Watson Howe

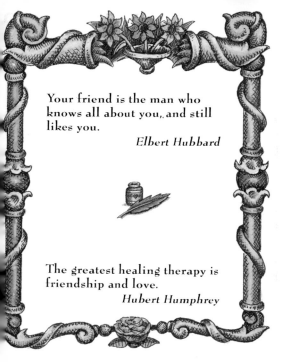

Your friend is the man who knows all about you,, and still likes you.

Elbert Hubbard

The greatest healing therapy is friendship and love.

Hubert Humphrey

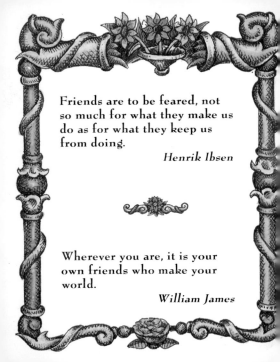

Friends are to be feared, not so much for what they make us do as for what they keep us from doing.

Henrik Ibsen

Wherever you are, it is your own friends who make your world.

William James

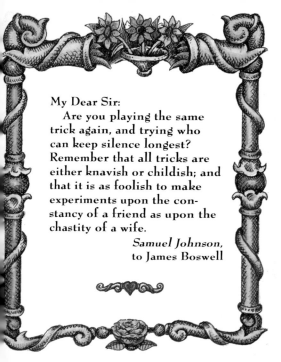

My Dear Sir:

Are you playing the same trick again, and trying who can keep silence longest? Remember that all tricks are either knavish or childish; and that it is as foolish to make experiments upon the constancy of a friend as upon the chastity of a wife.

Samuel Johnson,
to James Boswell

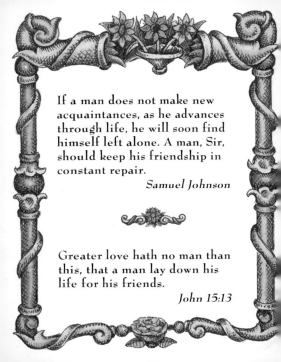

If a man does not make new acquaintances, as he advances through life, he will soon find himself left alone. A man, Sir, should keep his friendship in constant repair.

Samuel Johnson

Greater love hath no man than this, that a man lay down his life for his friends.

John 15:13

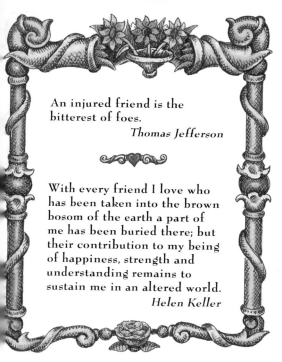

An injured friend is the
bitterest of foes.

Thomas Jefferson

With every friend I love who
has been taken into the brown
bosom of the earth a part of
me has been buried there; but
their contribution to my being
of happiness, strength and
understanding remains to
sustain me in an altered world.

Helen Keller

Real friendships must be
based on several shared
interests, so that when one
unravels, others remain.

Norman M. Lobsenz

Never while I keep my senses
shall I compare anything to
the delight of a friend.

Horace

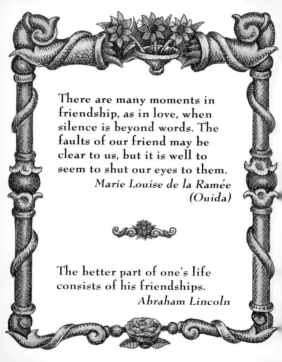

There are many moments in friendship, as in love, when silence is beyond words. The faults of our friend may be clear to us, but it is well to seem to shut our eyes to them.

Marie Louise de la Ramée
(Ouida)

The better part of one's life consists of his friendships.

Abraham Lincoln

Instead of a gem or a flower,
cast the gift of a lovely
thought into the heart of
a friend.

George Macdonald

I choose my friends for their
good looks, my acquaintances
for their characters, and my
enemies for their brains.

Oscar Wilde

When I was younger, I had more male friends than female friends. Now I've come to realize how rewarding women friends can be. There can be real love between girlfriends. That's something I learned from Nancy. She's always been there for me, and I'll always be there for her.

Donna Mills

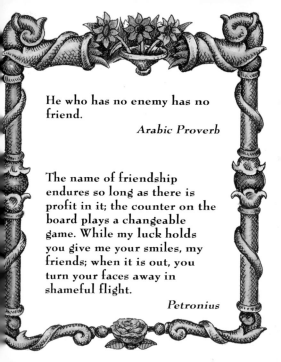

He who has no enemy has no friend.

Arabic Proverb

The name of friendship endures so long as there is profit in it; the counter on the board plays a changeable game. While my luck holds you give me your smiles, my friends; when it is out, you turn your faces away in shameful flight.

Petronius

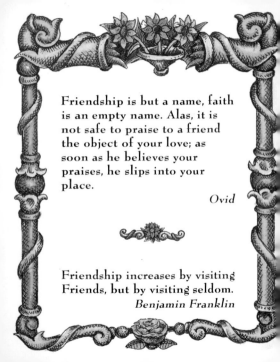

Friendship is but a name, faith is an empty name. Alas, it is not safe to praise to a friend the object of your love; as soon as he believes your praises, he slips into your place.

Ovid

Friendship increases by visiting Friends, but by visiting seldom.

Benjamin Franklin

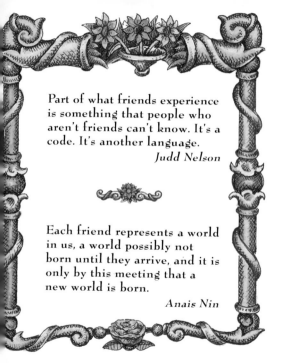

Part of what friends experience is something that people who aren't friends can't know. It's a code. It's another language.

Judd Nelson

Each friend represents a world in us, a world possibly not born until they arrive, and it is only by this meeting that a new world is born.

Anais Nin

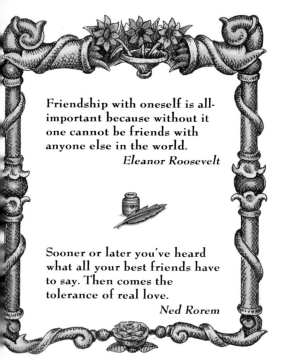

Friendship with oneself is all-important because without it one cannot be friends with anyone else in the world.

Eleanor Roosevelt

Sooner or later you've heard what all your best friends have to say. Then comes the tolerance of real love.

Ned Rorem

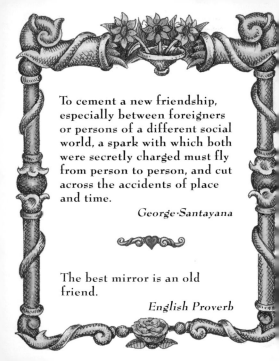

To cement a new friendship, especially between foreigners or persons of a different social world, a spark with which both were secretly charged must fly from person to person, and cut across the accidents of place and time.

George·Santayana

The best mirror is an old friend.

English Proverb

A friend in need, as the saying goes, is rare. Nay, it is just the contrary; no sooner have you made a friend than he is in need, and asks you for a loan.

Arthur Schopenhauer

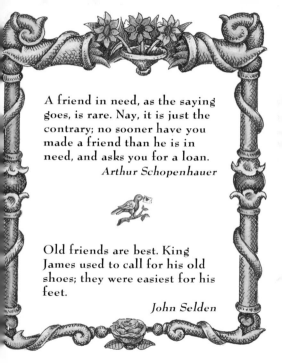

Old friends are best. King James used to call for his old shoes; they were easiest for his feet.

John Selden

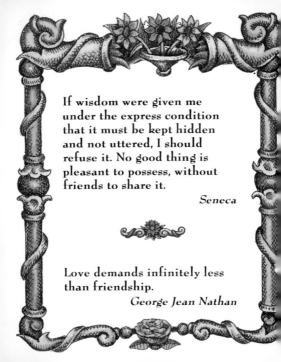

If wisdom were given me
under the express condition
that it must be kept hidden
and not uttered, I should
refuse it. No good thing is
pleasant to possess, without
friends to share it.

Seneca

Love demands infinitely less
than friendship.

George Jean Nathan

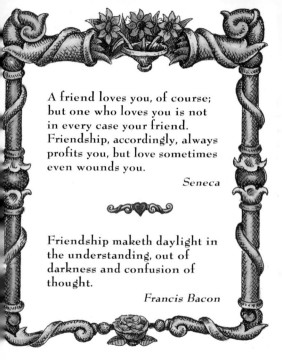

A friend loves you, of course;
but one who loves you is not
in every case your friend.
Friendship, accordingly, always
profits you, but love sometimes
even wounds you.

Seneca

Friendship maketh daylight in
the understanding, out of
darkness and confusion of
thought.

Francis Bacon

Treat a friend as a person who
may someday become your
enemy; an enemy as a person
who may someday become
your friend.

George Bernard Shaw

Keep thy friend
Under thy own life's key.

William Shakespeare,
All's Well That Ends Well

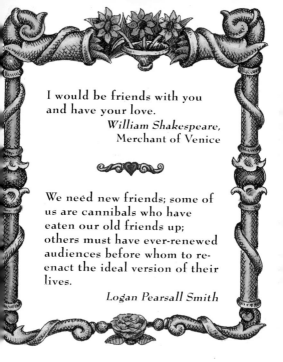

I would be friends with you
and have your love.

William Shakespeare,
Merchant of Venice

We need new friends; some of
us are cannibals who have
eaten our old friends up;
others must have ever-renewed
audiences before whom to re-
enact the ideal version of their
lives.

Logan Pearsall Smith

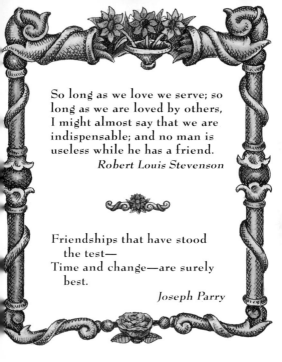

So long as we love we serve; so long as we are loved by others, I might almost say that we are indispensable; and no man is useless while he has a friend.

Robert Louis Stevenson

Friendships that have stood
    the test—
Time and change—are surely
    best.

Joseph Parry

No distance of place or lapse of time can lessen the friendship of those who are thoroughly persuaded of each other's worth.

Robert Southey

Believing that friendship may be retained by munificent gifts rather than by consistency of character, he should have had more friends than he did.

Tacitus

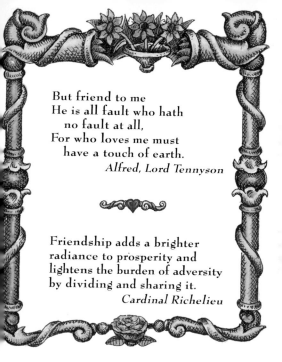

But friend to me
He is all fault who hath
no fault at all,
For who loves me must
have a touch of earth.
Alfred, Lord Tennyson

Friendship adds a brighter
radiance to prosperity and
lightens the burden of adversity
by dividing and sharing it.
Cardinal Richelieu

The holy passion of Friendship is of so sweet and steady and loyal and enduring a nature that it will last through a whole lifetime, if not asked to lend money.

Mark Twain

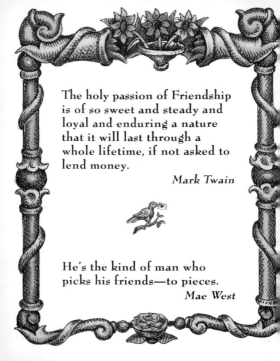

He's the kind of man who picks his friends—to pieces.

Mae West

One loyal friend is worth ten thousand relatives.

Euripides

Love is friendship set to music.

Edward Pollock

All men's friend, no man's friend.

John Wodroephe

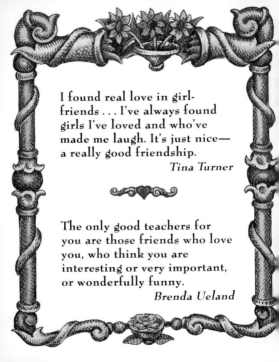

I found real love in girl-friends ... I've always found girls I've loved and who've made me laugh. It's just nice—a really good friendship.

Tina Turner

The only good teachers for you are those friends who love you, who think you are interesting or very important, or wonderfully funny.

Brenda Ueland

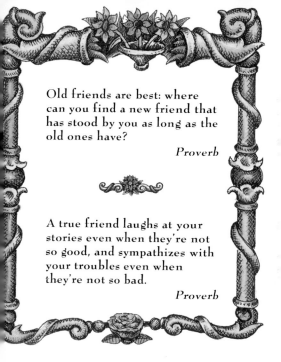

Old friends are best: where can you find a new friend that has stood by you as long as the old ones have?

Proverb

A true friend laughs at your stories even when they're not so good, and sympathizes with your troubles even when they're not so bad.

Proverb

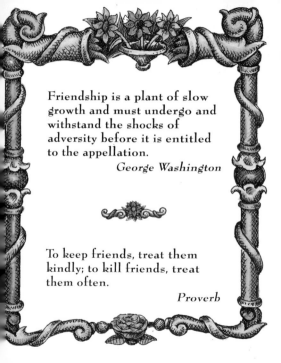

Friendship is a plant of slow growth and must undergo and withstand the shocks of adversity before it is entitled to the appellation.

George Washington

To keep friends, treat them kindly; to kill friends, treat them often.

Proverb

To go against the dominant thinking of your friends, of most of the people you see every day, is perhaps the most difficult act of heroism you can have.

Theodore H. White

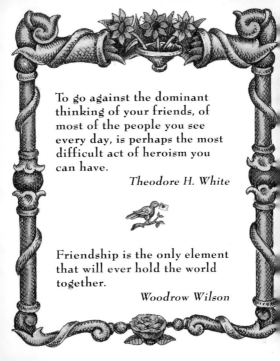

Friendship is the only element that will ever hold the world together.

Woodrow Wilson

You cannot be friends upon any other terms than upon the terms of equality.

Woodrow Wilson

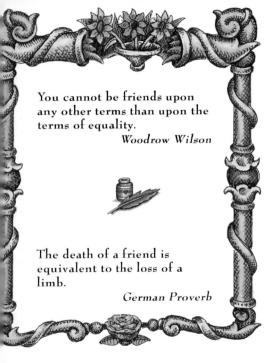

The death of a friend is equivalent to the loss of a limb.

German Proverb

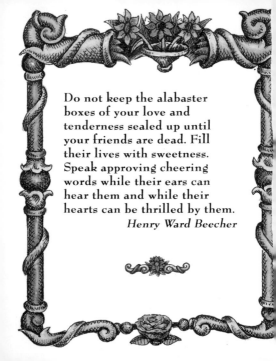

Do not keep the alabaster boxes of your love and tenderness sealed up until your friends are dead. Fill their lives with sweetness. Speak approving cheering words while their ears can hear them and while their hearts can be thrilled by them.

Henry Ward Beecher